·KINGFISHER·
KINGPINS

# The Superbook of
# STAMP COLLECTING

George Beal

## KINGFISHER BOOKS

# Contents

Kingfisher Books, Grisewood & Dempsey Ltd,
Elsley House, 24–30 Great Titchfield Street,
London W1P 7AD
This edition published in 1986 by Kingfisher Books
Reprinted 1989
© Grisewood & Dempsey 1986

Cover designed by the Pinpoint Design Company
Phototypeset by Southern Positives and Negatives (SPAN), Lingfield, Surrey
Printed in Hong Kong

Photo, previous page: J. Allan Cash
All other illustrations supplied by the author

BRITISH LIBRARY CATALOGUING IN PUBLICATION DATA
Beal, George
    Stamp Collecting.
    1. Postage-stamps – Collectors and
collecting – Juvenile literature
    I. Title
    769.56'075    HE6215

ISBN 0-86272-201-2

Opposite page: Aircraft make spectacular designs on stamps. Here is a selection showing an Avro F, 1912, two historic Russian aircraft, Concorde over London and over Paris, a stamp from the Isle of Man showing an RAF Jaguar, a Beechcraft machine over Norfolk Island, an Air Mauritius 'plane, a helicopter over New Guinea, and a stamp from Western Samoa commemorating the 50th anniversary of Lindbergh's flight across the Atlantic in 1927.

# Stamp Collecting

Stamp collecting has existed as a hobby for almost as long as stamps themselves have existed. The word *philately*, used to describe stamp collecting, first appeared in 1864 – when there were only about a thousand stamps in circulation! It comes from the Greek words *philo*, meaning 'a lover of', and *ateleia*, meaning 'free of payment'.

Stamps have a fascination which is difficult to explain to someone who is not a collector, but those bitten by the stamp 'bug' are usually addicted to them for life. It is a hobby which delights, excites, and is often profitable. Stamps are things of beauty (although there are a few exceptions). They are not difficult to store, and take up little space. If you are not a collector, we hope that your appetite for philately will be whetted by this book. If you are already a collector, we hope that, having read the book, you will feel that we have helped you.

# What you will Need

If you go into any stamp shop, you will be able to buy a 'stamp collector's outfit'. This will usually consist of some sort of album, a pair of tweezers, a perforation gauge, a magnifying glass, a packet of stamp hinges, a stock-book and a watermark tray. In fact, it is better not to buy a ready-made outfit. All of these items can be bought separately, and this way you can choose exactly what you want. The album will be the biggest item you will have to buy when starting out. There are many on the market, and you should choose the one that suits you best.

The tweezers are essential, for stamps should be handled as little as possible. Even apparently clean hands perspire, and there is nothing worse than an album full of grubby, dog-eared stamps. Perforation gauges are important, and the use of these is explained later in this book. A watermark tray is not quite so important a piece of equipment, unless you are looking at older stamps. You will find that most modern issues are unwatermarked.

However, a watermark tray is simply a small black dish, on which you place your stamp face-down, and then pour a tiny drop of benzine upon it. Any watermark will then show up quite clearly. Be careful with the benzine. It is inflammable – being a petrol-type liquid – and no naked lights should be present while it is in use. It is also very important to bear in mind that many modern stamps are printed in inks which are soluble in benzine, so recently-issued specimens should not be treated with it.

A magnifying-glass, on the other hand, is very important. Stamps are tiny things, and the detail on them is rarely easily seen with the naked eye. You can buy all kinds of magnifiers, some quite expensive, others reasonably cheap. The cheap ones are made of plastic, but they will usually serve well enough. Remember, however, that all magnifiers should be looked after carefully. Scratched lenses do not help you to identify the details on your stamps!

## Stamps and Inflation

In the 1920s, Germany was badly affected by inflation and banknotes and stamps had to have their face values changed constantly. Stamps with values of millions of marks were issued, then overprinted as their value decreased. A similar situation occurred in Hungary in 1945, when the pengö also became hugely inflated. Here are some of the stamps issued at those times.

# Where to get Stamps

If you want to collect stamps, there are a number of ways of acquiring them. You can buy them from all kinds of places; the local shop, a stamp shop, a jumble sale, from a friend, or by mail order. 'Local shop' sounds rather vague, but in some districts, a sweet shop or a stationers' will have packets of stamps for sale. Bookshops, especially second-hand ones, occasionally sell a few stamps. A specialist stamp shop is better, of course, but they aren't as easy to find as they once were. Jumble sales are worth going to, if you want a few odd stamps, but you will have to be prepared for some rather untidy boxes or envelopes. Another good place to buy stamps

▲ Definitive stamps are the standard ones usually on sale, as opposed to commemoratives, which are for special occasions. Some countries have an interesting theme for their definitive stamps. Left: four definitives from West Germany, showing a helicopter, a train, a mechanical digger and a tractor. Below left: an earlier West German definitive, showing Beethoven, one of a series of famous Germans; Italy, showing a coin of Syracuse, and two French definitives, the 'Sabine' head on the left, and the republican head on the right. Centre, top: four Austrian definitives from the series showing scenes from various districts. Centre, bottom: two Queen's head definitives, from Hong Kong on the left, and Great Britain on the right. Right, top: British definitives, showing variations for Wales, Scotland and Northern Ireland. The fourth is the standard version. Right: two Canadian definitives, a 3 cent stamp from the current USA series, and a South African definitive.

is at special stamp fairs. These are held in ordinary halls or rooms, and are normally open only on one day. Local newspapers usually publish details of where and when these are taking place.

# Mail Order

Stamps are also available for sale by mail order. You will find advertisements placed by mail order stamp dealers in many magazines. Buying this way is perfectly sound, if you know what you are looking for. This may seem obvious, but a very large number of beginners have no idea what to look for. Many dealers' advertisements offer free stamps. Such offers have an immediate attraction, but one must always bear in mind that nothing is really *quite* free. Dealers cannot go on giving away stamps

for ever, and when they do so, they expect something in return. That 'something' is, perhaps, your loyalty as a customer.

A common offer of free stamps is one in which you are asked to 'request approvals'. Stamps are sent out 'on approval' by dealers on the expectation that you will buy *some* of them. They are usually mounted up in book-lets, generally classified by countries or themes, and priced alongside. The customer who receives approval books or sheets takes what he or she wants, adds up the amount owed, and sends this off when the parcel is returned. This is quite a good way of getting special stamps, but it is fairly expensive. You have to pay postage, usually both ways, as well as for the stamps you have chosen. Mounted in books, stamps can look very attractive, and there is always a temptation to buy more than

◄ **Personalities on stamps:** Top row: Great Britain (Prince Charles and Princess Diana), USA (Ernie Pyle, wartime journalist), Great Britain (H.M the Queen Mother), South Africa (Robert Koch, bacteriologist), Congo Republic (Churchill). Centre row: Australia (Dame Nellie Melba, singer), Poland (Henryk Sienkiewicz, author of *Quo Vadis*), Mali (Newton), Great Britain (Nelson). Bottom row: St Pierre & Miquelon (President Pompidou), Poland (Eleanor Roosevelt), USA (Roosevelt), West Germany (Rubens, painter) and French Antarctic Territory (Cook).

you can afford. Another point always to bear in mind is that while the stamps are in your possession, you are responsible for them. If they are lost, stolen or damaged, then you – or your parents – will have to pay.

# Stamp Shops

When you visit a stamp shop, the dealer will almost certainly have bigger books of stamps, mounted up in a way rather similar to those sent out by approval dealers. The prices will be shown, and you will be able to decide exactly what you want as you see it. However, when you are starting out, visiting stamp shops, sending for approvals, and generally looking at single stamps or sets is not the best or the easiest way. Nearly everyone starting stamp collecting will take any stamps that come his or her way. It's very exciting getting them, but before long, you will need to decide exactly what you want to collect.

One of the most pleasant ways of starting is to buy a large packet of stamps – all different. Obviously, the price will vary according to the number of stamps in the packet. The best plan is to buy as large a packet as you can afford. Then, take the stamps home and sort them.

Apart from buying stamps, there are other ways of acquiring them. You can ask your friends to keep stamps for you. Relatives may receive envelopes from abroad, either at home, or through their business, and they will usually be happy to pass stamps on to you. Another way of collecting stamps is to join a stamp club. You can find out where your local stamp club is by enquiring at the desk in your library. All such clubs have a junior section. You can attend meetings, and they will usually have a 'club box' of swaps, through which you can expand your collection.

Stamps have to be stored somewhere. Once you have acquired your items, they will have to be mounted in an album. We shall discuss the matter of albums and other storage methods later. Very soon, you will find that you are getting stamps from all sorts of countries, but not enough to make a nice-looking arrangement in an album. You will soon realise that you can't collect every country in the world – there are just to many of them. Each year, something like 10,000 more stamps are issued, so the number gets greater as time goes on. You must decide what to collect.

### Mourning Stamps

Here are some examples of mourning stamps with black borders. The one from Belgium depicts Queen Astrid, who was killed in an automobile accident in 1935. The next stamp, from Greece, mourns the death of the US president, Franklin D. Roosevelt. The stamp from Yugoslavia commemorates the death of King Alexander, who was assassinated in 1934.

# What to Collect

Whatever you decide to collect, the most important thing to remember about stamps is their condition. You may decide to collect unused stamps, just as they were issued from the post office. Collectors who are concerned about the appearance of their stamps will usually collect unused ones. Despite the fact that stamps are produced to be used and postmarked, there are collectors who cannot bear to see any kind of blemish on their treasures. New stamps bought fresh from the post office will have no postmark, so they will be clean and new-looking, or what is known as 'mint'. Older stamps, even though not used for postage, can sometimes be in poor condition, due to bad handling. They may, for instance, have lost their gum. Nowadays, lots of collectors put great emphasis on this, rejecting or disregarding any stamp whose gum is not in its original state. Any stamp which is described as 'unused' must be in very good condition. Unused stamps will normally cost more than those which have been used. This is not always the case, since there are occasions when stamps have been issued and used only briefly before the issue was withdrawn. In such cases, used specimens will be rarer, and hence more costly.

Used stamps are more popular with collectors. They have, after all, performed the task for which they were intended; that is, to prepay the postage on mail. Many collectors will only collect used stamps, because they feel that unused stamps are not 'genuine' until they have done the job intended for them. Whichever way one sees them, used stamps are collectors' items, but they must be in good condition. They must be clean, complete, and only lightly postmarked. Scruffy, torn and heavily postmarked stamps are not worth collecting, and look unattractive on the album page.

It is possible to obtain stamps which have been postmarked or cancelled, but which still have their full gum. You may wonder how it is that a stamp can have been used and still be gummed in this way. The answer to this is that the stamp *hasn't* been used. What has happened is that the issuing country has deliberately cancelled whole sheets of stamps. The stamps are then sold off to dealers at a special price. The stamps can never be used for postage, but are classed as if they had been. If the gum is still intact, then it is easy to tell that the stamps have been 'cancelled to order', as it is termed. They are not prized as much as stamps used for postage. All the same, they are still collectable.

If you buy from a dealer, your stamps, if unused, will usually be 'off paper', which means you will be able to mount them directly into your album. However, sometimes, especially with stamps given to you by friends, they will still be stuck to the envelope. Don't try to tear the stamps off; you will almost certainly damage them. Stamps should be carefully soaked off their paper, preferably by laying them on to a sheet of damp blotting paper. You should be careful, since occasionally, stamps are printed with what are called 'fugitive inks', and the colours will run if the stamps are put into water. Also, be careful that dyes don't soak out of coloured envelopes or any other paper to which the stamps are fixed.

▼ Army uniforms shown on stamps: At left is a se-tenant block of four from Chile showing four different uniforms. Each of the stamps, however, has the same face value. At the top are four stamps from St Kitts showing British army uniforms, each stamp overprinted SPECIMEN. At the bottom are four stamps from Montserrat, also showing British army uniforms. Details of the uniforms are printed on each stamp.

◄ Several Slav countries use the Cyrillic alphabet in the inscriptions on their stamps. The first two here are from Bulgaria. Top right are two stamps from Yugoslavia, which was formerly called 'Kingdom of Serbs, Croats and Slovenes'. This is written at the top of the stamp (centre right) in Cyrillic, and at the bottom in Latin letters. Serbia was once a separate country, and issued its own stamps, as the example (right) shows. Below are examples of stamps from Montenegro and the Soviet Union. At one time, Ukraine issued its own stamps, an example being shown here (bottom right).

Some dealers sell what are called 'mixtures'. These are fat packets of stamps, said to be 'unsorted'. The stamps inside are still attached to their bits of envelope, and have to be soaked off. Usually, such packets are sold by weight, and contain lots of common stamps, but sometimes one can be lucky and find something unusual.

If you have been given a stamp on a complete envelope, don't be too hasty about soaking it off. Have a good look at the envelope first. It might have some interesting markings or stamped messages on it, or the postmark itself might be specially interesting. Such envelopes are best kept and collected as they are, being part of what is called *postal history*.

Most collectors decide to specialize. There are lots of ways of doing this. You can decide to collect just one country – perhaps your own. Or you can decide to collect a group of countries, such as those in the Common Market. Some people collect only stamps from English-speaking countries, since the inscriptions on the stamps are so much easier to read. However, there are many countries in this group today, and no one could expect to collect all the stamps issued by them. Alternatively, you can begin a *thematic collection*.

▲ After Austria was incorporated into Germany in 1938, stamps from both Austria and Germany were often used together on letters. Here is an example of two Austrian stamps with a German one in between, all on the same envelope.

► Flags on stamps. This is a popular subject for stamp design, as many countries like to show off their national flags on their stamps. At the top, the St Vincent stamp shows two flags (one being from Ontario, Canada), a Norfolk Island stamp with the Union Jack, a very large stamp from the Congo republic with 17 flags of African countries, and stamps from the Gambia and Togo each showing their own flag. Centre row: the British Virgin Islands and the Cayman Islands stamps have their own flag and the Commonwealth flag. Bottom row: the flags of Qatar, Haiti and China (Taiwan). One of the Taiwanese stamps also shows the flag of the United States of America.

# —Thematic Collecting—

Another very popular way of collecting stamps is according to subject matter. The subjects are called 'themes', and the branch of collection is called 'thematic'. What this means is seeking out any stamps which have been issued (or are about to be issued) on a subject or theme you have chosen. In America, thematic collecting is called 'topical' collecting. In this book, we have illustrated some examples of this kind of collecting.

You don't have to stick to one subject. There could be two or three collections, either linked, or quite separate. Here is a list of themes you might like to collect. All these subjects can be found on stamps.

Aircraft
Airships
Animals
Archaeology
Architecture
Coats of arms
Art and artists
Balloons
Butterflies and moths
Cars
Cats
Christmas
Costumes
Dogs
Explorers
Fishes
Flags
Flowers
History
Insects
Inventors

Maps
Monarchs
Music
People
Pets
Printing
Religion
Scouts and scouting
Sculpture
The Sea
Space
Sport
Stamps on stamps
Trains
Uniforms
Writers

# Collecting Covers

Covers are simply envelopes which have been used to contain something sent through the post. They are well worth collecting, and some people collect nothing else. People were sending letters to each other long before stamps were invented, and some of the early items are very interesting from a historical point of view. That is why they form such an important area in postal history. In the earliest days, individuals ran their own postal systems. In Britain, the state Post Office came into existence in the early 16th century. In those days, people had to pay varying rates for sending a letter; the farther it travelled, the more expensive it was.

▲ Japanese stamps are not easy to identify if the collector is unfamiliar with them. A clue is the value shown on this stamp in English as '6 SN.' (6 sen).

After the Second World War, Germany was occupied by the Allied powers: Great Britain, the United States, the USSR and France. The French zone issued stamps for each of the states of Baden, Rhineland Palatinate, and Württemberg.

◄ Stamps are overprinted for various purposes. At the top is a Montserrat stamp overprinted 'O.H.M.S.' (On Her Majesty's Service – an official stamp), a Taiwan Chinese stamp with the value cancelled with black bars, and stamps from Uruguay and Yemen both surcharged with a new value. Centre row: Another 'O.H.M.S.' stamp from Aitutaki, Cook Islands, a Pakistani stamp overprinted 'REVOLUTION DAY, OCT.27, 1959', two New Zealand stamps surcharged with a new value, and a St Kitts stamp overprinted 'SPECIMEN'. Bottom row: a stamp from the Turkish area in Cyprus overprinted 'ÖRNEK' (meaning 'specimen'), a Haitian stamp overprinted to commemorate Lindbergh's flight of 1927, an Indian stamp with the value cancelled, a Jamaican issue overprinted to commemorate Jamaica's airline, and a St Vincent stamp overprinted 'SPECIMEN'. Specimen stamps are issued to dealers, catalogue makers and others for information, but may not be used for postage. Sometimes, as above, the value is cancelled instead.

Such things are out of the reach of the beginner, but you can still form a most interesting collection of covers. The important thing is that there should be something special about the envelope. This could be an unusual handstamp, perhaps; or the letter could have been carried by an unusual method such as by airship. There could be an interesting or unusual array of stamps on the envelope. For example, when Hitler incorporated Austria into Germany, the Austrians still used their own stamps for a while, and it is possible to find covers with a mixture of Austrian and German stamps.

Today, the first-day cover has become very popular. Post offices – and many dealers – produce specially-printed envelopes to accompany new stamps, and the results can be very attractive. The envelopes are specially handled by the post offices, so that the postmarking and handstamping is done lightly and carefully. You can buy special albums made to hold such covers.

'Laibach' is another name for the Yugoslav province of Ljubljana. During the Second World War it was occupied by the Germans and Italians, and special stamps were issued. The earlier ones, as shown at the top, were overprinted Italian stamps.

# Postmark Collecting

Although it is unlikely to be your only practice, collecting postmarks can be an extremely interesting one. There are plenty of places with strange-sounding names, and one could make a collection just of those. Then there are slogans, such as POST EARLY FOR CHRISTMAS, or HAVE YOU USED THE POSTCODE? and many others around the world. Next time you handle any covers, have a look at the postmark, the slogan, or any handstamped markings. It is quite surprising what you will find. Unless the envelope is of special interest, the postmark, together with the stamp or stamps, should be cut neatly into a rectangular shape. Don't cut shapes around postmarks. It looks rather ugly. Plain rectangles look very much better. All you need then is an album to hold your specimens. The arrangement and classification of your postmarks is something you can decide for yourself; under countries, town names, or themes. Whichever it is, postmark collecting can be a very interesting sideline.

## Postal Stationery

Here are some examples of postal stationery. Illustrated is part of a postcard from the Netherlands Indies (now Indonesia), with a stamp printed on the card. Next is part of a postcard from Yugoslavia with the stamp printed on the card, although the design does not show a value. Also shown is part of a special card from Sweden, issued in honour of the 80th birthday King Gustav V.

The very first items of postal stationery were probably the Austrian *Korrespondenz Karte*, printed with a two-*kreuzer* stamp in 1869. In 1870 the British Post Office issued buff and violet-coloured cards imprinted with a half-penny stamp. These were sold at post offices and became very popular.

▶ This stamp, inscribed POHJOIS INKERI, was issued for the territory of Ingermanland, now part of the Soviet Union.

▶ Railways on stamps. Trains have always been a popular subject for stamp design. At the top are three trains from Tanzania, Australia and the Congo. Centre row: a steam train from Swaziland, an electric train from Belgium, an Austrian stamp showing the first electric tram in Austria, and a diesel train on a Tanzanian stamp. The bottom row is part of a set of stamps from Zaire showing interesting historical railway engines.

# Albums and Stockbooks

Once you have sorted out your stamps, you will need to keep them safe, and in a place where you can find them easily. The obvious answer is to mount them in an album. This is not the only answer, for there is such a thing as a stockbook. This is a book consisting entirely of blank pages, each with transparent pocket-strips arranged in rows. They come in various sizes. Stamps are slipped into the pockets and are held there until required, or can be left there more or less permanently. As their name suggests, stockbooks are intended for keeping stocks of stamps.

When you buy stamps, they have to be held safely until they can be mounted in an album, and the stockbook strips are very useful for this purpose. If they are unused, even a slight damp can cause the stamps in a packet to stick to each other. Separated out into the pockets of a stockbook, the stamps are safer.

There are quite a number of collectors who use stockbooks as albums. Provided the stockbook is of good quality, there is no harm in this. Stamps held in stockbooks do not look as attractive as those carefully mounted in an album, but it is a matter of personal choice. However, one should beware of very cheap stockbooks, since the plastic materials used in the strips can sometimes damage your stamps. Always buy from a reputable dealer.

◄ Examples of blocks of four stamps: from Japan, Romania, and France. The French stamps (which can be identified by the letters 'RF' in the top left-hand corner), were a Free French issue, as can be seen by the Cross of Lorraine in the top right-hand corner.

► Children's stories and nursery rhymes: left is a set of stamps from Tristan da Cunha. The designs show: *Little Jack Horner, Old King Cole, Mary Had a Little Lamb, Hey Diddle Diddle, Tom, Tom, the Piper's Son, Humpty Dumpty, London Bridge,* and *The Owl and the Pussycat.* Mickey Mouse and Minnie Mouse appear on two stamps from the Grenada Grenadines and Turks & Caicos Islands, while from Penrhyn comes a set illustrating Max and Moritz, from the comic verse by the German poet and artist Wilhelm Busch.

The majority of collectors will keep their stamps in an ordinary album. Again, these vary enormously in size, scope and type. If you have bought a large packet of mixed stamps, you will probably buy an album with pages printed for all the various countries in the world. The pages will have squares marked out for the stamps, so all you have to do is to sort your stamps into countries.

The result will be quite attractive. You may find, however, that the majority of your stamps are just odd ones. Most stamps form parts of sets or series. For instance, the definitives of Great Britain (the standard stamps with the Queen's head) make a very pretty show when together, but you may have perhaps, only about half of them. If you buy more, you will want to keep them all together, and in sequence. You will find that the printed album will not have enough spaces for even the recent issues of Great Britain, let alone just the definitives. What are you to do?

It is at this point that you start making decisions about specializing in one or more countries, or even starting a thematic collection. If you decide to collect only certain countries, you will need special albums for them. Again, there is a choice. There are blank albums, with loose leaves, or albums with spaces especially marked out for the stamps of the countries you are collecting. These are

quite expensive, and new pages will have to be bought each year, in order to make room for the new issues of the countries. The best idea is probably to buy a good blank album, and to arrange the stamps on the pages youself. With a little thought, you will be able to make good arrangements. Then all the items on the page must be labelled. This is called 'writing up'. If you are very clever with your pen, you can do this by hand. Alternatively, little books with printed country-names and philatelic wording can be bought, and stuck down in the right positions. Instant-transfer letter systems can also be used, but this requires some skill if the final result is to look attractive. Another way of labelling pages is with a typewriter, if one is available. All the names, words, dates, figures, etc. should be neatly typed on good paper, and then pasted down into position.

▲ The world's first adhesive postage stamp was the One Penny Black, issued by Great Britain on 6th May, 1840. A Twopenny Blue was issued two days later. Since that time, five other monarchs have reigned in Great Britain, and here we show stamps depicting each of them.

# Mounting Stamps

Everyone nowadays knows that real stamp collectors do not stick their stamps into albums with paste or gum. In the early days, collectors actually did such things. If your grandfather or some elderly relative makes you a present of an old stamp album, 'handed down' from some previous collector in the family, think yourself lucky, for old albums sometimes contain treasures. But if you found some interesting old stamp, only to discover that it was fixed on to the page with gum or glue you would be very upset! Yet that is exactly what one often finds with old items. Fortunately, the idea of mounting with peelable stamp hinges has been with us for some time now, so many early albums will have properly mounted specimens.

A stamp hinge is a small piece of semi-transparent paper. To mount a stamp, a small strip is folded over at one end of the mount with the gummed side outwards. This turned-over strip is then moistened, and placed at the top of the stamp to be mounted. A small area of the other end of the mount is also moistened, and this is then applied to the page in the position chosen. When dry, the mount can be peeled easily from the page, or from the stamp. This is the theory, and it works – except in the case of unused stamps! Naturally, any gum on such a stamp will become moistened along

## German States

Until the early part of this century, Germany was split up into a number of independent or semi-independent states, each of which issued its own stamps. Here are some examples from Prussia, North German Confederation, Thurn and Taxis, and Saxony. Bavaria is called 'Bayern' by Germans. This state became part of greater Germany after the First World War and its stamps were overprinted DEUTSCHES REICH ('German realm'). Heligoland was once a British possession, but was ceded to Germany in 1890. The stamp shows the head of Queen Victoria, but the currency is shown in pence *and* in pfennigs (German coinage).

▲ Foreign alphabets and scripts. Some stamps are difficult for beginners to understand because they use unusual alphabets. Here are a few; top row: China (Chinese script), Korea (Korean alphabet), India (Devanagari script), Yugoslavia (Cyrillic and Latin alphabets), and Laos (Laotian script). Centre row: China (Taiwan) showing Chinese and English inscriptions, Bulgaria, showing a newspaper in Cyrillic script, Yemen (Arabic script), and Japan (Japanese script). Bottom row: USSR (Cyrillic script), Turkey (two stamps) showing the old Arabic script and the modern Latin script, Greece (Greek alphabet), and Sri Lanka (Sinhalese script).

◀ This stamp of Austria, issued in 1922, appears to be simply a very modernistic design, with the representation of a face in the centre. In fact, it is a portrait of a real person. She was Erica Wagner, an Austrian opera singer.

with the hinge, and once mounted, the hinges are not nearly as peelable.

In fact, many collectors refuse to put hinges on to unused stamps. Special protective mounts (or 'pochettes') are often used instead. These come in transparent strips of varying height, to allow for different sized stamps. Strips are cut into widths to fit the dimensions of the stamp, and then the stamp is slipped inside the pochette. One side of the mount is gummed, and this is fixed to the album page. The stamp is totally protected. Some pochettes come with a black backing, and stamps mounted in this way can look very attractive, but the mount must be cut carefully, to leave an equal margin all round.

# How Stamps are Produced

Like most other printed products, stamps are first designed by an artist. He usually works to a size larger than the actual dimensions of the stamp. When the design has been approved, it is sent to the printer to be processed. Stamps are printed by a number of methods, but the main ones are called letterpress, engraving, photogravure and lithography. You may wonder why it is necessary for collectors to know about such things. The reason is that, quite apart from pure interest, collectors need to know how to distinguish one stamp from another. For instance, the definitive stamps of Great Britain are normally printed by the process called photogravure, but occasionally,

certain stamps have been printed by the lithography process. At a glance, a stamp printed by one method will look very much like one printed by another. Collectors, however, will want to have examples of both.

▼ **Airships and balloons. Top row: Liberia (Graf Zeppelin), Uruguay (LZ-127 Zeppelin), Bulgaria (balloon ascent at Plovdiv, 1892), Mongolia (Mongolfier balloon, 1783). Centre row: Romania (airship over Paris, 1901), Romania (British R34 airship over New York, 1919), Mongolia (Graf Zeppelin, 1931), Congo Republic (balloon in Jules Verne's story *Five Weeks in a Balloon*), West Germany, from a set showing a balloon over Munich, 1820, a Zeppelin in 1900, and a flying machine in 1909.**

# Letterpress Printing

This is the simplest of all printing processes. The design, or *image* is applied (in reverse) to the surface of a metal plate, and the blank parts are etched away. This leaves the design part in relief, or standing up. Ink is then applied to the surface of this upraised part, paper is pressed on to it, and a print is taken. The result is a single-colour reproduction of the design. If the design is to be in more than one colour, then extra metal plates are made, each of which is used to produce a single colour. Printing takes place in a high-speed press, and each single colour plate is printed on to paper in sequence.

# Photogravure

This process is a form of mechanical engraving produced by photographic means. It is cheaper than engraving proper, and a more graduated design is possible. Instead of lines produced by the engraver, the photogravure plate is built up from tiny cells etched into a copper cylinder. This cylinder is used for printing, and when it is inked, and the surface scraped clean (as with engraving), a fine print is produced. Many-colour photogravure printing is possible, the final product being a very richly printed stamp.

▲ The first French issue of 1849 showed the female head known as 'Ceres'. This was changed when Louis Napoleon became president in 1852. His head simply replaced the female one. Meanwhile, other countries had begun to issue stamps, and many looked at the French design and unashamedly copied it, changing only the details of the country and other wording. Here we have examples from Norway in 1856, showing the head of King Oscar I, and a detailed copy from Greece in 1861, showing the Hermes head. Another very close design was issued by Romania in 1872, showing the head of Prince Carol.

▼ One day in each year is set aside as the 'Day of the Postage Stamp', and in some countries, special stamps are issued. Here are examples from Germany in 1944 and 1983, and from Austria in 1983.

**Bilingual Stamps**

Andorra is a small country in the Pyrenees, and both France and Spain have an interest in its government. Two kinds of stamps are issued; one bearing French inscriptions and currency, and the other Spanish. Here is an example of each kind of stamp, together with similar examples from Canada and South Africa. For many years, Belgium issued stamps with a small tag at the bottom. The tag is in the two official languages of Belgium, French and Flemish, and means NOT TO BE DELIVERED ON A SUNDAY. If the sender wished the letter to be delivered on a Sunday, he simply tore off the tag.

# Lithography

This is now the most widely-used method of printing stamps. The artist's design is photographed, and then printed down photographically on to a specially-prepared sheet of metal. This sheet is then placed into a chemical bath rather similar to that used when photographic films or prints are processed. The result is a black image of the design upon the surface of the sheet of metal, known as the plate.

The image is neither engraved into the plate, nor is it raised from the surface. The plate has a special character, in that when ink is applied to its surface, it 'takes' only in the areas on which the image is seen. The ink remains on the design, and not on the other areas. The plate is thin and flexible, and is wrapped on to a roller in a printing machine, making a printing cylinder. Ink is then applied to the cylinder-plate. When the machine starts, another rubber cylinder comes into contact with the cylinder-plate, which 'off-

▶ **Flowers on stamps. Top row: St Vincent (Purple-Throated Carib), Lesotho (Wahlenbergia undulata), Morocco (Malope tripida), Papua New Guinea (Dendrobium bracteosum), West Berlin (floribunda), Switzerland (lungwort). Centre row: Philippines (Mussaenda Dona Hilaria), Ascension (bougainvillea), Mauritius (Dombeya acutangula), West Germany (red clover). Bottom row: Australia (waratah), the Gambia (Clerodendrum splendens), Botswana (Ammocharis coranica), St Christopher-Nevis-Anguilla (Canna coccinea), Congo Republic (Nympheas micrantha).**

▲ This pair of Swedish stamps comes from a booklet, and perforations were not needed at each edge. They are therefore *imperforate*.

# Engraving

The finest stamps are printed by the engraving process. Again, the design is produced by an artist, but the processor engraves the design *into* the steel. This is called a *die*, and when it is finished, the whole pattern is reproduced, as made by the artist. This die is then specially hardened and is used to make a number of identical impressions onto softer steel, making up *plates*. Ink is applied to the crevices, and a special knife-blade sweeps across the surface, taking away any surplus ink. Paper is applied to the plate, and a print is taken, the ink, of course, coming from the recesses, and not the surface. The result is a very fine print of the design. As with the letterpress process, other colours can be added by producing extra plates.

sets' the design. The rubber cylinder, now being inked with the design, in turn prints on to the paper.

As with the other printing methods, many duplicate copies of the design are produced on the plate together, so that a number are printed at one time. Extra colours are printed as the paper passes through the machine.

◄ After the end of the First World War, the Austro-Hungarian Empire was broken up, and some of its stamps were overprinted DEUTSCHÖSTERREICH for use in the new country of Austria. Later, stamps with that inscription in the design were issued.

► The Greek alphabet appears on Greek stamps, on those of Cyprus, and formerly appeared on stamps from the island of Crete. The first stamp has the name LORD BYRON in English, and the stamp commemorates the help given to the country by the English poet. At the top of the stamp is the word ELLAS (meaning 'Greece') in Greek characters, with the value showing 2 DR (drachmae). The Greek inscriptions on the second stamp, put into Latin characters are ELLAS (Greece) and 50 LEPTA (which are Greek coins). In the bottom row are two modern stamps from Cyprus, one commemorating the 13th European Games in 1982 and one Vasilis Michaelides, a Cypriot poet.

# Paper

Very good quality paper is used for printing stamps. Until fairly recently, stamp paper was 'watermarked' to prevent forgery. Watermarking is done less frequently nowadays, but older stamps have them. They were added during the production process. Paper, when it is being made, is a pulp having something of the appearance of a thin porridge. It dries on a wire gauze surface, and watermarks are produced by wire patterns placed into the gauze. This produces a thinning of the paper in those areas, which show up as watermarks in the finished paper.

# Perforations

When stamps were first issued they had to be cut out with scissors. The tiny holes found today between each stamp and its neighbour are called *perforations*, and almost all modern stamps are produced in this way. However, perforating stamps is not the only way of making them easy to pull apart. There is also a system called *rouletting*, which involves making a series of tiny cuts in the paper. Rouletting can be straight, or use zigzag or even curly cuts, but the idea remains the same.

Perforations vary quite a lot. The holes themselves can vary in size; the distance from

◀ The little area of Campione is part of Italy, but is actually situated inside Swiss territory. In 1944, the commune issued its own stamps, one of which is illustrated here. The stamps were used until 1952.

▲ A recent fashion has been to print the design of an earlier stamp as part of the design of a new one. Usually these show some sort of stamp anniversary, as do the three at the top. Centre row: The first four stamps commemorate the birth centenary of Sir Rowland Hill (who first thought of the stamp), while the stamp from the Cook Islands has five stamps reproduced. Bottom row: commemoratives for Sir Rowland Hill from Sri Lanka, Botswana and the Gambia, and an Irish stamp showing an early American stamp design.

◀ In the days of colonial rule, special companies were sometimes set up to run overseas territories. Here are some examples of the special stamps which were issued by these companies.

▲ Bosnia and Herzegovina once issued stamps on their own account, although they were part of the Austro-Hungarian Empire. No country names appear on these two stamps, but the date is significant, as is the portrait of the Archduke Ferdinand of Austria, whose assassination led to the First World War. At the end of the war, the two provinces became part of Yugoslavia, and stamps of Bosnia, and Herzegovina were overprinted like that on the right.

▼ The English name for a foreign country is often quite different from the name used in the country concerned. Here are some stamps showing examples of this difference: MAGYAR KIR is 'Hungary', and the overprinted word KÖZTARSASAG means 'republic'. The word on the other stamp, MAGYARORSZAG, means 'Hungarian country'. Earlier this century, Turkey was called the Ottoman Empire, and stamps were inscribed 'Postes Ottomanes', in French.

one hole to the next also differs, according to the machine used; and there are two ways of making the perforations. One uses a line of pins, making a single row of holes, which moves along the paper. The other uses a grid of pins, which chops all the holes at one time. The first is called *line perforation*, and the second *comb perforation*.

Stamps with different types of perforation are regarded as different. The perforations are measured with a perforation gauge, which measures the number of perforation holes within a distance of two centimetres.

Occasionally, stamps are issued without perforations, although it is rare. Sometimes the perforating machine misses a sheet or part of a sheet, in which case, the stamps will be *imperforate*. It is well worth examining a sheet to see if any perforations are missing. Such stamps are very much sought after by collectors, and have a higher value.

► Ships have been used on stamp designs almost from the very first issues. In the top row are stamps from Paraguay, Tuvalu, Hong Kong and Austria. Centre row: a river steamer (Australia), a cargo vessel (St Pierre & Miquelon), a passenger liner (Bahamas), and a fishing boat (New Zealand). The bottom row shows four sailing ships: from the French Antarctic Territory, Bulgaria, the Cayman Islands and Poland.

# Stamp Catalogues

One essential piece of equipment for any stamp collector is a stamp catalogue. Many people think that a catalogue is something you consult only when you want to know the value of a stamp. This is rarely the case, and the prices shown in such a book are really the publisher's idea of what stamps are likely to cost if you buy them. Most catalogues are published by stamp dealers and are a sort of dealer's price list. Other dealers may not agree with those prices, and can sell at a greater or lower price if they wish to. Also, buying and selling stamps are two quite separate operations. If you buy a stamp at, say, a catalogue price of £1, and try to sell it a few weeks later, you would be unlikely to get anything like that figure. Dealers are in buisness to make a profit, and stamp dealing today is a somewhat hazardous affair, so there must be a fair profit if a dealer is to survive.

The stamp collector uses a catalogue to find information about stamps. You may acquire a

The world's most valuable stamp is the British Guiana 1 cent issue of 1856. Only one example of this stamp exists, and although it is not for sale, the value is probably in the region of £600,000.

◄ Some stamps have had advertisements printed on the back, and some stamps in booklets have small advertisement labels printed alongside. Other issues have advertisements printed in the margin of sheets. Here are some Italian stamps issued in the 1920s, with an advertising label attached. Also illustrated is part of a sheet of German stamps issued in 1922. The margin at the right has been used for advertising. Also shown is a British example from the 1930s.

► Sport on stamps. Top row: Mongolia (skiing), Vietnam (throwing the hammer), Bulgaria (weightlifting), Swaziland (soccer), Antigua (cricket). Centre row: Malta (sailing), USSR (riding), West Germany (fencing), Burundi (long jump). Bottom row: Czechoslovakia (cycling), Liberia (figure skating), Solomon Islands (boxing), Israel (lawn tennis) and Finland (volleyball).

rather attractive stamp. You look it up, and find that it forms part of a set of similar stamps, in which case you try to complete the set. A catalogue will say when the stamp was issued, and who designed and printed it. Naturally, you will also be interested in the catalogue value. It is always exiting to find that a stamp you already own has a good value in the catalogue. But never get too excited! The stamp is not actually 'worth' that price; it is usually what a particular dealer will sell it for.

Catalogues list stamps under countries, dates, colours, types and face values. The face value is the amount shown on the stamp. A British stamp may have 20p shown upon it, which is its face value, and if the stamp is available from the post office, it will cost you

► For a short time after the First World War, the city of Danzig was a 'free city', and issued its own stamps, like this airmail issue.

◀ Croatians speak a language which is almost identical with Serbian, but the Croats use the Latin alphabet. Slovakia, now part of Czechoslovakia, uses a language almost identical to Czech, but written in the Latin alphabet, so stamps were inscribed SLOVENSKÁ POŠTA. The united Czechoslovakian republic inscribed its stamps ČESKOSLOVENSKO.

20 pence. If the stamp is no longer issued, you may have to buy it from a dealer. He will almost certainly charge you more than 20 pence for it. The famous British Penny Black was originally sold at one penny, but it will cost you a great deal more than that today!

Stamps are also listed under the colours in which they are printed. A large number of stamps today are printed in 'multicolour'.

Modern printing machines are able to print many colours at one printing operation, and such stamps are often very attractive. However, there are still plenty of stamps printed in one colour only, particularly definitives. Catalogues may describe a stamp as, say, '4p green', and right next door to it, is another entry, '4p blue-green'. These are two different colours, but how are they to be distinguished by the collector? This is done by using a colour guide, available from dealers, and especially made for stamp collectors.

There are all kinds of catalogues on sale today. You can buy simplified volumes containing details of every country in the world, or you can buy others which specialize in just one country or a group of countries. Naturally the simplified catalogue – large though it may be – will not contain the amount of detail found in a specialized one.

Beginners do not need the detail that more experienced collectors require, so the all-world simplified catalogue will be right for them. However, catalogues are not cheap, and few beginners are prepared to spend a lot of money to buy one. Most public libraries now have copies of the major catalogues, which you can borrow. They may not be totally up-to-date,

but they will give you quite a lot of the information that you need. Catalogues come out – with some exceptions – every year. When the new ones appear, some dealers will sell off the previous year's catalogue, perhaps at half-price. It is worth keeping a lookout for such items at the time when the new ones are issued.

▼ Stamps come in many shapes and sizes. Here are a few strange ones: top row: a Mongolian diamond-shaped issue, and a similarly shaped stamp from the USSR. In the centre is a stamp from Norfolk Island actually made in the shape of the island. These come in sheets, but the actual stamps are self-adhesive, and are peeled off the backing. Centre row: An oval design from Mexico, rhomboid and triangular issues from Mongolia, and a tiny half-sized stamp from South Africa. The bottom row shows another triangular stamp (from Ecuador), a self-peel stamp (with no perforations) from Tonga, a book-shaped design from Liberia, and an imperforate stamp from Austria.

# Terms Used in Stamp Collecting

▲ Here are examples of three Turkish 'bisects'; that is, stamps which have been cut in half for postal use when there was a shortage of certain values. They have been overprinted with a new value.

**Adhesive** Stamps with a sticky back. The word is usually applied to ordinary postage stamps, compared with stamps printed or embossed on to envelopes.

**Airmail** Stamps specially issued for use on letters or other items sent by air. Only certain countries have done this; others use ordinary postage stamps with an *airmail label*.

**Bisect** When stocks were short, some post offices in some countries took higher value stamps and cut them in half diagonally. Each half was then used to prepay postage on mail.

**Block** Four or more unsevered stamps retained as a rectangle, as opposed to a *strip*, which is several unsevered stamps in a row.

**Booklets** For convenience, stamps are sold in small booklets. These stamps are sometimes different from those sold singly.

**Cachet** A handstamp or printed inscription on a cover giving some special information, such as publicizing an event or date.

**Cancellation** Any mark used to deface a stamp on a postal item to show that it has served its postal purpose. The mark is usually an ordinary postmark.

**Cancelled to Order** Stamps which have been especially cancelled in bulk by a postal authority in order that the sheets can be sold to dealers at a lower price. Such stamps will not have actually passed through the post.

**Chalky paper** A specially-surfaced paper coated with chalk, used for printing stamps. Forgers were sometimes able to clean off postmarks, but this was not possible with chalky paper.

**Christmas Seals** Stamp-like labels sold at Christmas-time for charity. They are not stamps, and serve no postal use.

### Booklets

Illustrated here are the covers of two booklets from Switzerland; the top one containing the 'Pro Juventute' charity stamps, and the lower one the normal definitive. Booklets are usually collected and kept in the condition in which they are issued.

◄ 'Essays' are not stamps, but designs for stamps. Only a few are actually accepted for issue. Here are two Mexican essays which never became stamps. They show the emperor Maximilian, who was shot before the stamps could be issued.

**Coil stamps** Stamps specially printed in long coiled strips for use in machines.

**Commemorative** A stamp issued to mark some special occasion or event.

**Counterfeit** Another name for a *forgery*.

**Cover** An envelope, wrapper or other covering for an item sent through the mails.

**Definitive** A stamp issued for normal, everyday use, and usually available for an unlimited period.

**Demonetized** Stamps which are no longer valid for postage.

▼ Insects on stamps. Top row: Rwanda (honey bee), Great Britain (stag beetle), Falkland Islands (mayfly), Central African Republic (Drurya antimachus butterfly). Centre row: Cuba (Colosoma splendida beetle), New Caledonia (agrianome beetle), Rwanda (corymodes beetle), Vietnam (damsel-fly), Maldives (Memnon butterfly), St Vincent (Red Antavtia butterfly), and Mongolia (Parnopes wasp).

## Key Types

Here are some examples of 'key type' stamps. The basic design remains the same, only the name-plate and the face value at the bottom varying according to the colony. At the top are some examples of British colony key-types and some from the Malayan states of Sungei Ujong and Selangor.

Below are some 'Yacht' key types used for the former German colonies of the Caroline Islands and Togo; French colonial key-types; the 'Ceres' key-type used for Portuguese colonies; and a Spanish 'Baby' key-type intended for the former colony of Cuba.

**Die** The metal on which a stamp design is engraved, and from which multiple copies are made for printing.

**Duplicates** Extra examples of a stamp already in one's collection. All duplicates should be closely examined for minor variations. They can then no longer be regarded as duplicates.

**Embossed** A design raised in relief. Stamps have been produced like this, but embossed designs are usually found on envelopes.

**Error** A mistake made in producing a stamp, or in the original design.

**Essay** A design produced for a stamp, but which was not subsequently used.

**Fake** A genuine stamp which has been altered or 'doctored' in some way in order to deceive collectors and others.

**Flaw** A minor variation in a stamp design, which is usually only seen on a limited number of stamps in the printing run.

**Forgery** A deliberate and fraudulent imitation of a stamp. 'Postal' forgeries are intended to deceive the post office, and 'philatelic' forgeries are intended to deceive dealers and collectors.

  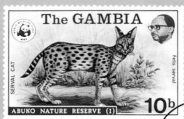 

## Local Stamps

Local stamps are issued either officially or privately to pay postage in a limited or local area. Between 1840 and 1866, there were many local stamps issued in the United States. Issuers of some worked in co-operation with the official post office, while others were in competition. Some of these stamps are illustrated here. Also shown are a German local issue, and a local stamp issued in the Channel Islands before the post office had issued their own.

◄ Mammals on stamps. Top row: Mauritania (elephants), Rwanda (chimpanzees), Poland (wolf), Kenya (giraffe), Seychelles (bat), Tanzania (hartebeest), Guyana (manatee), the Gambia (serval cat), St Christopher-Nevis-Anguilla (green monkey), Liberia (leopard), Vietnam (palm civet), Malawi (buffalo) and Botswana (pangolin).

**Gum** The adhesive applied to the back of stamps. *Mint* stamps have the original gum in a perfect state.

**Gutter Pair** Two stamps connected at the centre by the white paper called the 'gutter'.

**Handstamp** A postmark or other mark on a piece of mail applied by a hand-held stamping device.

**Hinge** A small piece of semi-transparent paper, gummed on one side with a special adhesive which will 'peel' when dry. Hinges are used for mounting stamps in an album.

**Hotel Stamps** Local stamps issued by certain hotels in Europe. They were used to pay a fee for carrying the mail of residents to the nearest post office.

**Imperforate** Stamps printed in a sheet without perforation holes, rouletting or other aids to separation.

**Imprint** The printer's name, as it appears on a stamp or sheet.

**Inverted** Something in the design or on the overprint of a stamp which is turned upside-down.

**Kiloware** Parcels of mixed stamps sold by weight.

**Local Stamps** Stamps issued either officially or privately to pay postage in a limited area.

**Magnifier** An optical instrument for viewing stamps.

**Map Backs** Stamps printed on the backs of German war maps issued by Latvia in 1918.

**Maximum Cards** Picture postcards on which a stamp has been placed; the stamp having a design similar to, or related to, the picture on the card.

**Miniature Sheet** A sheet of stamps containing fewer stamps than the normal sheet, sometimes with just one stamp.

**Mint** A stamp in perfect condition, exactly as issued by the post office.

**Mounts** Items used for mounting stamps. See *hinge* and *pochette*.

**Mourning Stamp** A stamp issued to commemorate the death of someone, often printed with a black border.

**Muster** An overprint found on German stamps. The word means 'specimen'.

**Newspaper Stamps** Special stamps issued for paying postage on newspapers.

**Obsolete** Stamps which are no longer available from the post office. See *Demonetized*.

**Official Stamps** Stamps specially issued for use by government departments or individuals.

## Omnibus Issues

Omnibus issues are stamps which often have the same design, but which are issued by a number of countries. The Silver Jubilee of King George V of Great Britain was an occasion for stamps to be issued in all the British colonies. Here are examples from Hong Kong and Mauritius.

▼ Here are examples of overprints and surcharges. 'POSTES PERSANES', as shown on the first stamp, is French for 'Persian Post'. When the name of the country was changed to Iran, this word was overprinted on the older stamps. An overprint which changes the face value of the stamp is shown on the stamp from Papua. Also illustrated is a Russian stamp surcharged 20 paras for use in Russian post offices in the Turkish Empire.

▲ British Somaliland, a former British colony in Africa, had no stamps of its own until the stamps of India were overprinted for use there. Sometimes, ordinary British stamps were overprinted for use in colonies or countries abroad. Here are some intended for use in British post offices in Morocco.

**Omnibus Issue** A group of stamps, usually with the same or a similar design, issued by a number of countries to commemorate a particular occasion.

**Overprint** Something additional printed upon a stamp.

**Parcel Post Stamps** Stamps specially issued for use on parcels sent through the mail.

**Pen-Cancel** Stamps cancelled by the use of a pen.

**Perfins** Stamps which have been punch-perforated with the initials of a firm or some other organization, to deter the theft of stamps.

**Perforation** A series of holes punched between rows of stamps to aid their separation. See *Rouletting*.

**Philatelist** Another name for a stamp-collector.

**Phosphor** Stamps are often inked or printed with phosphor lines or bands in various combinations. These lines glow under ultra-violet lamps, and are 'read' by a special scanner which separates first from second-class mail.

**Pochette** A small pocket-shaped stamp mount made of transparent plastic, sometimes with a black backing.

**Postage-Due Stamps** Labels fixed to letters to show an amount due on a letter or package which has not been stamped, or which has insufficient postage stamps for the purpose.

▶ 'Se-tenant' stamps are those which are joined to their neighbours on the same piece of paper but which are in some way different. Top row: five stamps from Syria with different face values and designs. Centre row: two Canadian and two British stamps with different designs. Bottom: these three Christmas stamps from Norfolk Island actually form part of the same picture, but when the stamps are detached from each other, they form separate pictures. Right are two more Canadian stamps, both 17 cent face value, but with different designs.

**Postmark** Any mark made on a package or envelope by a postal authority, giving date and origin of the item concerned.

**Precancels** Stamps with cancellations already applied by machine are used by large firms who post their mail in bulk.

**Propaganda Forgery** A stamp forged during wartime, not for postal use, but as propaganda.

**Provisional** A temporary issue of stamps put out until a more permanent issue can be made.

**Rouletting** A method of making staggered cuts or slits in the paper between stamps to aid separation, as an alternative to perforation.

**Se-tenant** This phrase is French for 'joined together'. It is applied to two or more stamps which are unseparated, especially when the design on each stamp is different in some way.

**Sheet** A complete 'page' or single printing of a stamp. The number of stamps on a sheet can vary from about 240 down to 30.

**Surcharge** An overprint which alters or confirms the face value of a stamp.

**Sweat Box** A safer way of soaking paper off the back of stamps. This is an airtight box containing a pad soaked in water, over which is a metal tray with holes in it. Stamps adhering to paper are placed on the tray, then left until the paper becomes detached.

**Tête-bêche** A French expression which refers to a stamp or stamps in a sheet printed so that two stamps are joined with one upside-down in relation to the other.

**Thematic Collecting** Collecting and arranging stamps by the subject or theme depicted in the design rather than by the country of origin.

BERLIN - 50 JAHRE AVUS-RENNEN 1921 - 1971

▲ This stamp from Czechoslovakia was issued in 1948, with labels also printed in certain positions on the sheet. Such labels, se-tenant with the actual stamp, are much sought after.

◄ This miniature sheet was issued in West Berlin in 1971 to commemorate the 50th anniversary of the Avus motor-racing circuit. Four stamps of different values and designs are printed together.

◀ Motor-cars and motor-cycles. The top row shows four stamps from a set issued by Mali illustrating veteran motor-cars. The centre two rows are from West Berlin, being Youth stamps issued in 1982 and 1983 showing early cars and motor-cycles. They are overprinted 'MUSTER', which means 'specimen'. At the bottom are three stamps, the first from Swaziland, and two others showing motor-cars from East Germany and the Congo.

### Hitler Heads

During the Second World War, definitive German stamps bore a picture of Hitler. Allied propaganda experts made a deliberate forgery of the 12 pfennig value, but instead of the normal portrait, the stamp showed a 'death's head' skull. The words DEUTSCHES REICH were changed to read FUTSCHES REICH ('the Reich is lost'). It was hoped that this stamp might find its way on to letters in Germany. This is an example of a *propaganda forgery*.

**Tied** When the postmark on an envelope or other postal item extends beyond the border of the stamp, it is termed 'tied'.

**Tweezers** An essential piece of equipment for any stamp collector. Stamps should always be handled with good-quality tweezers.

**Ungummed** Stamps are sometimes issued without gum on the back. This happens either by mistake, or more likely, in warm countries where the gum is likely to melt and cause the sheets to stick together.

**Unissued Stamps** Stamps which have been printed and prepared, but never issued. This may have been because the design was con-

sidered faulty, or because some political change had taken place.

**Unused** A stamp that has not been employed for postal use. A *mint* stamp is unused, but the term is usually applied to stamps which have been mounted with hinges, so that the original gum has been impaired.

**Used Abroad** Stamps used in countries other than the country of origin. In earlier times, for instance, some British stamps were used in places such as the West Indies. They can be identified only by the postmark.

**Variety** A stamp which differs in some visible way from a normal specimen. This is usually caused by a fault in the printing process.

**Watermark** A thinning of paper which will show up when the paper is held up to the light.

▲ An example of a pen cancellation (in this case a simple cross) on an early Canadian stamp. Before Canada became a dominion, the various states issued their own stamps. Here also are examples from Nova Scotia and Prince Edward Island.

# Index